YOUR STORY

IS NOT

YOUR STORY

From Adversity To

SUCCESS

Through The Hardship Of Life

Lucas L. Armstrong

ISBN:149286353X
ISBN-13:9781492863533

DEDICATION

I would like to dedicate this book first to my God; without him none of this would not be possible. I would like to thank my moms, Martharine Ollison and Jackie Delph, for never giving up on me and my dreams, also my dads, Earlee Armstrong and Cleroy Ollison, for showing me lifelong learning experiences. I cannot forget Jeffery Brown who always stuck by my side and was always there for me, teaching me how to be a man and a father. Last but not least, I dedicate this book to my kids Jaylon, Saniah, Keyonte, and Akeyla for giving me the inspiration to go toward my dream because I always wanted a better life for them.

To: Thomas

Keep moving Sir!!!

[illegible]

CONTENTS

INTRODUCTION

One key to successful leadership is continuous personal change. Personal change is a reflection of our inner growth and empowerment.
—Robert E. Quinn

Through my story I want people to understand that in order to have success you must grow personally in all areas of your life. It does not matter what you have gone through but that you grow through it. I want you to know that your story is all you have, and nobody can take that away from you. If you have a dream, don't give up on it; and if God has put it in your heart and your dreams, then it's already done. Life will happen to you but through your own personal growth you will succeed and impact the world.

My mission is to let you know that I believe in your dreams, but you have to understand that you have it in you already to have the life you want. Remember, it's not over until you win. I believe in you, so go live your dreams. Take care and God bless.

YOUR STORY IS NOT YOUR STORY

CHAPTER 1
THE MIRACLE CHILD

I came into this world fighting for life as a premature baby weighing only one pound. My mother lay in her hospital bed as the doctor told her that they had done all they could because of my conditions as a premature baby. The doctor basically left me for dead, saying that her newborn was probably not going to live past three years old because I was not fully develop as a baby . Thankfully my mom was a fighter: she prayed all night, hoping everything would turn out for the best. I have been fighting for my life ever since.

Growing up I heard everybody say that I was a lucky child, a miracle that God had me here for a reason. This put a lot of pressure on me as a young child. Even at a very young age I knew my life had to be great because of how I was brought into this world.

As a premature child things were difficult for me. Back then they would put you in a category signifying that something was wrong with you mentally or physically. My mom said that I was very quiet in that I did not eat at all during those times. All I remember was going to the doctor, being tested all the time, and hearing the doctor say to my mom, "Your son might have lots of problems as he gets older."

So at this time in my life I knew I was a miracle child and that God had me here for a reason. I didn't know why I was here; I just knew that I would do big things in my life.

At that time a major thing happened in my life: my mom left my dad because he was cheating on her with other women. My parents got a divorce but a strange thing happened: my dad got custody of my brother and me, and my mom just disappeared from our lives. I was lost and confused, crying every night, wondering what happened? Why did my mom leave us? I was upset at my mom, and that pain hurt me for a long time. What happened, and how could a mother leave her kids like that? It took me a while to understand why my mom left.

That was only the beginning, because at times, I would fault my mother for some of things that happened in my life. It took me growing up and asking for forgiveness toward my mother, the lady who treated me like an angel when I was a younger.

After the divorce, my mom let our dad get custody of us. Being the older brother, I always felt like I had to protect my brother.

CHAPTER 2
LIFE WITH MY DAD

My dad was not ready to settle down or raise his two little boys. He had other kids but we were the only ones who lived with him. There were times when we would stay with other people because my dad was always gone or doing whatever he was doing at that time in his life.

I always felt lonely and by myself, with no one to talk to—just sitting there quietly, always wondering why we could not be with our mother. My mother had other things going on in her life because she had two daughters who lived in a foster home. I never knew what that was about. My brother and I would visit them at the foster home, but the whole time I was thinking, "Where is my mother? "

Years later my sisters told me things about my dad that really broke me down as a human being, things that happened while my mom and dad were together. So growing up I had to put a lot of things together in my head. I figured that my mom had to find out who she was as a woman, and that she had to get away in order to find herself in the world. Even so, I was confused and there were some things I would never forget.

Staying with my dad as I was growing up was one of the worst periods in my life. Not only was I confused and wondering what was going on with my life, but I also thought things could not get any worse.

The things that happened during this part in my life affected how I lived and destroyed my self confidence as a person and as a man. As I am writing this book, it's hard to explain some of the things I went through because it took me a long time to forgive my dad for things he did.

When a child does something wrong you may spank the child or use some words to make him or her understand that you mean business. But it's another thing when you take your shortcoming out on your child because things are not going the way you want them to. Seeing my dad disrespect my stepmother and doing things he had no business doing affected how I perceive my dad as a father. He physically abused us, beating us with the water hose and anything else he could get his hands on.

It felt like I could do nothing right. I was slapped down so many times that I would jump every time I was around my dad because I that he would find anything to hit me with. He would pull a plant out of the ground and beat me with it, just for not moving fast enough or not working the farm the way he wanted. People felt sorry for us, but no one said anything. My dad bragged to his friends and other people about how he had beaten us, while laughing like it was funny.

I remember one incident in particular because I thought I was going to die. We were cutting the grass and the lawn mower stopped working. I tried my best to fix it, but my dad took his rage out on me and hit me in the head with a wrench. My brother also had marks on his face because my dad hit him with a switch. Through all of that my dad never said that he was sorry for anything that he'd done.

Those things changed my life forever, and I knew that I could never be the man my dad was while my brother and I were growing up in those early years.

In addition to abusing me, my dad thought I was slow because of my premature birth, and he also thought that I was mentally retarded. He'd come to my school to see how I was doing, and the teacher would say, “Your son does not understand any of the work that I’m teaching.” So my dad took me to all of these psychologist, or, as I put it, “crazy doctors.” My dad kept telling me I was slow and that I would never amount to anything in life. As a young man that hurt me deeply, especially when I found out he was just trying to get government funding for me. But that never happened because I passed the doctors’ tests.

During that time in my life I had no confidence and often thought about suicide, to just leave this earth. I was mad at God. I believe I was supposed to be this miracle child. Why did he have me going through all of this mess in my life?

Eventually my mom came back in the picture. When my brother and I were a little older she would pick us up on the weekends and give me and my brother that motherly love. It was a time to escape the things that were going on with my dad. I was happy because my mom had really found herself and seemed to be very happy in her life. Unfortunately her baby boy was not happy.

My dad did not have much money because the farming business was seasonal. There were many days when my brother and I had no food or clothing. We would always go to our grandmother's house to eat. One time our water had been cut off and we had to steal water from the church to wash ourselves off. We sat in a dark house many days because the electricity was off. This would be a driving point for me when I got older: never to go through things like I did when I was younger.

After all the bad things my dad did to us he did teach me something, it was the sport of basketball. This activity became an outlet for me to not think about the things that was going on in my life. I like the sport so well that I joined the local team. Happy and excited that he introduced this to me I just knew he would be my #1 fan… boy was I wrong. He never came to many of my games.

It seemed like I was moving along with no guidance and no one to turn to. I would sit on my basketball late at night, wishing on a star, saying that I would be famous one day and that my life would not be like this anymore. Many nights I cried myself to sleep, praying that everything would get better and that life would not always be like this. Early on I began with the end in mind, and I also kept a mental vision of how I wanted my life to be.

CHAPTER 3
WORKING ON THE FARM

I started working on the farm when I was six years old. My dad grew vegetables and in the summertime, he would hired people who could not find a job or who needed extra money. Just imagine: beginning at six years of age, I got up at five thirty in the morning during the summer and while school was in session.

I learned how to work, and I also learned how I could help people who really needed help. My dad would get old people to work for him; they would tell the stories about how they messed up their life due to drugs or by making the wrong choices. Those stories motivated me to have a better life.

Unfortunately it was still a bad time for my brother and me. Our dad took everything out on us for any mess-ups that happened. We were just kids; we did not know anything about farming or running a business. My dad abused me in front of the people that he hired. It was embarrassing, getting slapped so hard that it would send me to the ground in front of everybody. The people working for my dad would tell me to stay strong. "One day you will grow up and it will be over," they said.

I also learned an important lesson from my granddad, the first man to ever tell me that he loved me. The lesson was that you should always get something on your own when you get older, rather than working for someone else, because you can call your own shots.

My brother and I always cried and said that we would never return to the farm, but the farm taught us how to work and not to work for anyone else in life. I carried that work ethic we me to do all I could to accomplish my goals and also live through the people who would or could not live their dreams because of their choices. I felt it was my duty to make it for myself, and to make it for them too. I carry that pain and their advice in my heart all the time.

CHAPTER 4
A BOY TO A MAN

Another turning point in my life occurred when I was in the tenth grade. My dad was in jail because he failed to pay child support. He'd also done some bad things on the streets. All the bad things he had done finally caught up with him. I had to learn how to be a man early because my dad was in jail. It was just me, my stepmother and my brothers and sister.

I worked with my granddaddy on the farm, picking peas and selling them so we could pay the bills at the house. I got another job so I could help out and pay for my own clothing.

During that time I got cut from my high school basketball team. I didn't give up on my dreams, though I moved to a different high school to accomplish my dream of playing high school basketball.

I remember having a conversation with some of my classmates. We got to talking about our lives, and I told them all the stuff I'd been through. They were almost in tears. I told them that early in my life I learned how to smile through all the pain I'd been through I learned that trouble don't always last.

After high school I went to college to study business marketing. I remember having a conversation with my dad; he told me bluntly that I would not graduate from college. That lit a much-needed fire under me. When times got hard in college I did not quit because I always remembered that conversation.

During this time I had my first son, and even though I wanted to be this big businessman I was forced to grow up quick because I now had a child. During college I got a job working at Wal-Mart as a cashier.

At Wal-Mart I met a guy who would change my life forever. His name was Lawrence Owens. Before I met Lawrence I always talked about having my own business and becoming a millionaire. This man showed me what it was to be a father. He took care of his family and did everything to give them the best life. I was impressed with the way he carried himself. He was a gentleman and a man with class.

The most important thing he did was give me a CD that introduced me to the world of personal development. That information change me as a person.

I started my own business at the age of twenty-two and had success very quickly. I had a chance to learn from a millionaire who embraced me for what I had been at an earlier age and who was there for support. Despite all of this, I still had a lot of personal development to do within myself.

Also during that time I met my best friend and the man I call my angel here on earth. His name is Jeffery Brown. He was a great asset and huge positive influence to my life. He is a business owner from my home town. When I had no money to take care of myself, he was there to help me. He was always there when I needed him, and he always believed in my dream to be a successful person who would impact the world.

CHAPTER 5
THE GRADUATION

I kept my promise to my mom that I would be the first child in my family to graduate from college. I got my degree in business marketing because I still wanted to be that big business man one day.

My dad, the one person who said I would not graduate, did not come to my graduation. Two of his kids received their degrees that day, and he was nowhere to be found after promising my sister and me that he would come. That hurt me as a son, but what did I expect from a man who never told me he loved me and never apologized for what he did to me when I was younger?

I got my degree and came home and said, "Mom, here is your degree," because she always wanted to go to school but things happened and she did not complete that part of her life.

CHAPTER 6
THE CAR WRECK

Soon after I graduated—the next day, in fact—my life changed forever. I was in a car accident. It's crazy because before I left that night to take my daughter and her mother home, my mom and my stepmother told me that something compelled them to get up and pray.

I was driving them home when I saw a parked car that I thought belonged to a friend of mine. Being the person that I am, I pulled over to take a look. It wasn't my friend's car. I saw a man and a woman walking away from it. They had run out of gas.

I asked them what happened and if they needed some help. They said yes. I moved my sleeping daughter from the back seat up with her mother in the front, and the man and the woman got in the back. The last thing I heard them say was, "That's a pretty little girl!" and "Thanks for picking us up."

I started the car and was trying to get back into the highway when a speedy drunk driver hit the back of my car. My daughter and her mother were ejected from the car, and the two people I was helping also flew out of the car. I jumped out and saw that the mother of my daughter was on the side of the road. She'd been knocked unconscious but she was okay.

I looked for my daughter. I saw her lying on the road, and I ran to pick her up. She was not moving. I immediately started praying to God. *Please don't let my little angel die!* All of a sudden she started moving really fast. I said, "Daddy is here, daddy is here."

I did not see the other people but I found out later that they were dead. God had everyone in place that night to save my little family. There was a paramedic behind us that night he said that normally he would be home but got into a deep conversation with his sister and he was the one working on my daughter. An undercover state trooper was also behind us. After we got hit by the drunk driver, he kept going as if nothing had happened.

I had to learn how to forgive myself for what happened that night because at times I felt like it was my fault. In my mind I see the scar on my daughter's face, and I feel like I put it there. I know her life outweighs those feelings but every time I see her I think of that night that changed our lives.

When I say that personal development is the key to life, I really mean it. When the accident happened I had no one to talk to, but the positive information that I put in my mind help me to get over the pain I had in my heart. One of the relatives of the guy who was in my car said that she forgave me, but she added that she wanted me to do something big in my life. From that point I was compelled to do just that and pay my respect for the lives that were lost. I could not settle for an average life.

CHAPTER 7
THE CANCER

Several years after the car wreck I was hit with something else that hit me hard in my life. My youngest son was diagnosed with cancer. Until that point I figured that God had built me to handle different problems in my life.

We believe that he was not going to live long. His mother took it very hard because everyone who had cancer in her family had died from the disease. Working on my mind-set prepared me for this situation because I never thought, *He's going to die.* I just thought, *Hey, we are going to get through this* and that he is already fine.

For the next two years my little boy battled cancer and all the things that came along with it. I am happy to say that today he is cancer-free and is living a normal life.

At this point I asked God, "What's going to happen now?" It seemed as if I had been going through things since I was born into this world.

I remember hearing a little voice inside of me saying, *Your story is not your story. It's for other people to hear your story, to help them in their lives.*

CHAPTER 8
THE MOVE

I went after my goals and kept my promise to the family member of the guy who died in my car that night. I moved to Dallas, Texas, with somebody whom I thought could help me become a successful businessman. I was happy and excited about my future. Though when I arrived in Dallas I found out that I did not have anywhere to stay.

I'd put my trust in some millionaires who lied to me about coming to stay with them. I was dating this young lady at the time, and her parents found out what happened and through the grace of God, they let me stay with them. Staying with them allowed me to see what family is all about, because growing up I never had a family with my mom and dad.

Eventually I moved into my own apartment and got a job to take care of myself. I didn't earn much pay but I really needed it. In the back of my mind I felt like a failure because nothing was going right in my life as I'd planned it. I never gave up on my dreams, so I invested all of the money I had to get my business started.

Along the way I met some people who could help me in the areas where I needed it. The first of my mentors was a guy named Johnny Wimbrey. He was an international speaker and author whom I patterned my speaking career after. He taught me things that I'll cherish for the rest of my life and it was mostly just looking at him impact the world. During this time I was learning and working on myself as much as I could, just waiting for that opportunity to give my story to the world.

Another life-changing event happened at my job that really shook my world and instilled faith back into me, my lifelong dream of becoming a speaker and impacting the world with my story.

One night when I was at work I heard a loud noise outside in the parking lot. I ran out there and saw two young girls lying on the ground. Suddenly I had a flashback to my car wreck, so I ran to one of the young girls to see what had happened. One of the girls was slumped over in a tree, and the other girl was in the middle of the parking lot. Both of them had been ejected from their car.

I went to the young girl who was in the middle of the parking lot. She was conscious. I held her in my arms and told her, "I am not going to let you die." I prayed to God, saying, *Not again. I don't want to see someone's life flash in front of my eyes.* Through God's grace and mercy both of the sisters survived the life threatening car wreck and credit me for saving their lives.

At that time in my life I was living from paycheck to paycheck. I had no food and was eating turkey sandwiches and cereal to survive. I slept on an air mattress and listened to audio books and read positive books, telling myself that I would make it big one day.

I wanted to go after what I always wanted to be a person who would impact the world through my story with persistence and consistency, never giving up on my dreams. So I quit my job and found a mentor who could help me reach my dreams.

CHAPTER 9
THE JOURNEY BEGINS

I wanted to paint a picture of my life so you would understand that life has its ups and downs, but that you should always remain focused on having a successful life. It took eight years for me to make peace with my past, to find out what I wanted to do with my life. Was it hard? Yes, it was, but through consistent and focused effort I finally made it over the other side.

People ask me all time about how I overcame the physical and mental abuse and the deaths in the car wrecks. I tell them, first, God; next, self development, because that's all I had to turn to. I learned early how to change my thinking and my environment by reading positive information or listening to things that could change my life.

At times I wanted to give up, but I remembered when I was little and my mom said that God had put me here for a reason and that reason was to impact people. My gift of loving people and to want them to succeed is my passion, and it makes me so happy to have people overcome their past and succeed.

I had a revelation when God told me that my story was not my story and that it was for other people to help them with their lives. So that made it easy to deal with my past and to move forward in life.

People are not going to believe what you have to offer to the world, but if God put it in your heart, then it must happen. But you have to take that step to work on yourself at all times and understand it is a process to be successful. It does not happen overnight.

Now I go all around the world telling my story and helping people grow to be better people so they can achieve their goals. I not only impact them with my story, but I also let them know that we all go through things in life. Willey Jolly, the first motivational speaker I heard, said that a setback is a set up for a comeback. You have comeback power, and through self-development you will receive your breakthrough.

In order to do something great you have to become a different person than who you are now. Through self-development a new person can grow out of you and you can impact the world with your story. Don't give up; just remember when things happen to you it's just God testing you to see how bad you wanted it.

One last thing: I want you to know, your struggles are blessings from God, and that your mess can become your message to the world.

CHAPTER 10
SELF HELP TIPS THAT CHANGED MY LIFE

Personal development is an ongoing process, but this action plan will give you some of the things that helped me deal with all of the mess that I had in my life and actually changed me into the person I am today.. In order for you to have success in your life, you must develop yourself in all areas of your life. This will be a complete guide on how to change right now, by learning from my years of experience.

I advise you to take action immediately because life is short and you don't have a whole lifetime to change your life or to be successful. Trust me, if these principles can change me into the man I have become, I know without a doubt they can change you. I BELIVE IN YOU

LIFE LESSON 1

MENTAL CLEANSE OF YOUR MIND-SET

The thirty-day mental fast is a way to help you clean your mind-set of all the deprogramming or negative things in your mind.

These steps should be used for thirty days in a row to fully experience the change that is going to take place in your life.

Step 1. No TV

Turn off the TV for thirty days. Why? Because there is so much negative programming on TV. This step applies especially to people who watch the news at night before they go to bed. That's why a lot of people have a lot of fear in them. Fear means "false evidence appearing real." Why watch other people live their dreams on TV while you're sitting at home, not living yours? Please keep out the number one negative TV station in the world and that is Constant Negative News. NO TV.

Step 2. No Radio

Do not listen to the radio while you are driving to work unless it is something positive. There is nothing in the morning that's positive that you are listening to. When you turn on the radio, what do you hear in the morning? Somebody is having a wreck, or somebody is spreading some gossip. You want to be stress-free before you go to work, not depressed because you heard some bad news on the radio. In addition, most people do not want to go to work because they hate their jobs. That's too much for one person to handle. NO RADIO.

Step 3. No Newspapers

What you read is going into your mind-set. So why put the negative front page into your mind-set? Newspapers have a lot of disempowered information that make you scared to do anything. The first thing you see on the front page is who got killed or robbed, and all the bad things that are going on in the world or in your city. If there is bad news, trust me, you don't have to read it. Somebody will tell you about it. NO NEWSPAPERS.

<u>Step 4</u>. Read Positive Books

There are so many good things to read that can help you change your life. Instead of picking up a newspaper, pick up something that will inspire your life. Read at least thirty minutes a day. Here are some books that have changed my mind-set: *Think and Grow Rich, Outliers*, and *The Greatest Secret in the World.* READ POSITIVE BOOKS.

<u>Step 5.</u> Listen To Positive Audio

In Step 2 we said don't listen to radio because we want to change your "internal radio" to an empowered radio station. There are so many great motivational speakers in the world who have great information for you. So every time you turn on your radio, put in a positive CD and relax your mind to another level. These are a few of the people that I listen to on a daily basis: Les Brown, Brain Tracy, Anthony Robbins, and Denis Waitley. LISTEN TO POSITIVE AUDIO.

Step 6. Exercise

A lot of people get scared when they hear the word *exercise*. So for thirty days, just do a little more movement. Find a parking spot that is farther away, so you can walk to work. Instead of taking the elevator, take the stairs. When you get home, take a walk around the block. Just take at least fifteen to thirty minutes a day to do some type of movement. By exercising you release a lot of tension and stress that comes from being around a lot of negative people.

Step 7. Reflection

This is the time you can reflect on your day or go over your goals. You can also use this time to pray and to give thanks for your life. Remember, always take out time for yourself. Before you can take care of somebody else, you have to take care of yourself. REFLECTION .

These are the steps that will help you transform your mind and get rid of all that negative garbage in your life. Remember, if you want to have wealth in all areas of your life, you have to start with your mind.

LIFE LESSON 2

UNDERSTANDING YOUR INNER SELF

Attitude

It does not matter what happens to you in your life. When it comes down to business you must have a great attitude to handle all the success and things that come your way. The people who make the big money have a great attitude because they handle big problems that other people could not handle.

Gratitude

There are a lot of people who are not grateful for the things they have. That's the reason why they do not have the things they want. It does not matter if good or bad things come your way.

Emotions

A lot of people have not learned how to control their emotions. If something happened to them in their past, they hold onto their emotions, which keeps them from progressing toward their future. Let it go so you can flow.

Work Ethic

When it comes to work ethic, you must be able to work hard in every aspect of your life and business to be successful.

Motivation

You have to learn how to motivate yourself when things are not going your way in life or business. You have to stay hungry at all times.

Relationship

Develop good relationships with anybody and everybody you come in contact with in your life. Remember the old saying: Treat people as you want to be treated.

LIFE LESSON 3

THE FUNDMENTALS OF LIFE

These fundamentals are vitally important in determining how well we perform at certain stages of our lives. How well you master them will determine how prone you are to errors in your performance.

Faith

Someone outside of yourself is here helping you here on earth.

Commitment

To commit firmly to whatever it is that you set out to accomplish and to remain focused in the face of opposition, with the end result in mind.

Concentration
Your ability to focus and perform without being distracted.

Efficiency
The more efficient you are, the less effort you will need to perform. The less effort used, the more strength you will have later in the game. An efficient performer sometimes feels like a well-oiled machine. Bottom line: how efficient you are is determined by how effective you are at producing results.

Consistency
Successful people develop good habits, and they hold to their principles. The more consistent you are in your performance, the more reliable you will be to others.

Persistence
When I think of persistence, I think of doing something over and over and over again. I see persistence as not giving in because of opposition.

Perseverance
I think of perseverance as doing something more and more, as in "coming back for more." The ability to persevere is to continue doing something in spite of obstacles or difficulty in accomplishing your goal.

Execution
Your level of performance will be determined by how well you execute your plans. Execution is defined as how well you perform according to your plan.

Determination
To make up your mind that nothing will stand in the way of achieving your goal.

Hard Work
Hard work will not hurt you. A willingness to put forth maximum effort at all times is the best way to describe hard work.

LIFE LESSON 4
PRIORITIES

Happiness is a successful combination of all areas of your life. Establish what is important and commit to it. Creating balance in your life is a necessity. The road to the mountaintop is a rough one. There's a lot to remember and a lot to do along the way. It all takes time and energy, and sometimes it seems like there aren't enough hours in a day to do what we should do. It can seem like a juggling act to balance all the demands of our time.

I believe that the only way you can be totally happy and effective in any area of your life is to set priorities equally in all key areas. Remember the four areas: family, spiritual, work, and recreation. By structuring your life to include each one of these areas, you can reduce anxiety.

LIFE LESSON 5
THE POWER OF A BIOGRAPHY

A biography has amazing potential power. In it lies the hidden button that, when pushed, can be used to unleash the power within you—the untapped, resource that you alone possess.

There is an art to reading a self-help book. When you read, *concentrate*. Read as if the author were a close personal friend and is writing to you alone. Before you read a self-help book, determine what you are looking for.

If you know what you are looking for, you are more apt to find it than if you don't have a specific purpose. If you really want to recognize, relate, assimilate, and apply success principles that are contained between the covers of an inspirational book, you must work at it.

You have to pull ideas from successful people until you reach your own success. Here are some steps to apply:

Read for general content. This is the first reading. It should be a fast reading, to grasp the sweeping flow of thought that the book contains. But take the time to underline important words and phrases. Write notes in the margins and briefly write down the ideas that flash into your mind as you read. Now obviously this may only be done with a book that you own. But the notations and markings make your book more valuable to you.

Read for particular emphasis. A second reading is for purpose of assimilating specific details. Pay particular attention to see that you understand and really grasp any new ideas the book presents.

Read for the future. This third reading is more of a memory feat than it is a reading task. Memorize passages that have particular meaning to you. Find ways they can relate to problems you are currently facing. Test new ideas, and discard them unless they leave a useful, indelible imprint on your habit patterns.

Read late to refresh your memory. All of us may become discouraged. We should re-read the best of our books at such times to rekindle the fires that got us going in the first place.

LIFE LESSON 6
YOUR PURPOSE

The purpose of your life is far greater than your own personal fulfillment, your peace of mind, or even your happiness. It's far greater than your family, your career, or even your wildest dreams and ambitions. If you want to know why you were placed on this planet, you must ask God, then take action. You were born by His purpose and for His purpose.

LIFE LESSON 7
LUCAS'S 7 KEYS TO WIN IN LIFE

1. Decide on your purpose
2. Find your niche
3. Do right, then everything else will be right
4. Reward yourself
5. Use life experience as a teacher for you
6. Don't use your own thinking all the time
7. Life is short, enjoy the moments

LIFE LESSON 8

DREAM BOOK/ GOAL SETTING

If you want to start having success, taking your goals from your head and putting them on paper is the key.

When you write down your goals you need to break them down into five areas: physical, spiritual, financial, career, and relationships.

These are the questions you need to ask yourself when you have written all your goals down in those five areas:

1. When would you like to accomplish each of these goals?
2. Select your top three goals—the ones you are committed to accomplishing right now.
3. List the character traits you need to accomplish your goals.
4. What do you feel are the road blocks that keep you from you accomplishing your goals?
5. What are you willing to give to accomplish your goals?

Invent your ideal day and be specific, from the time you awake up until the time you sleep.

The next step is to take all your goals and create a dream book or dream board. Cut out your dream house and dream cars and paste them on a board. For you can look at every day to keep you focus. Break down in detail everything possible you may want or you need in life.

LIFE LESSON 9

PAY THE PRICE

Nothing worth having comes easy. The most successful people realize this. They are willing to pay the price, and that's why they are living their dreams. In our daily lives we recognize the fact that big dreams have big prices. We must determine the price we're willing to pay for success.

Many people want a fast, easy road to success, but there isn't one. The harder you work, the luckier you become. You have to work your butt off to stay on top. It's all about paying a price to be the best. In other words, I don't want anybody handing me things.

Please remember: the greater the rewards, the greater the price. There are those who think that some people are just born lucky or that they get handed everything. That's not true. Everyone has to pay a price of one kind or another. There are some people who don't look at life as a challenge. They refuse to compete, refuse to work hard, and aren't willing to pay a price for success and achievement.

I think those people end up paying a price after all: a price for not competing, and a price for not trying to become the best that they can be. I believe that their price is not feeling good about themselves: not having dreams or ambitions, not having financial security, not being able to do things they want to do for themselves and their families. In my opinion, this is the saddest kind of life and the biggest kind of price.

Paying a price builds confidence and staying power. When you really work hard and sacrifice, it builds both your mental attitude and your ability to do something well. When you really work hard and you're really prepared, you develop an expectation of winning. You know you're ready. You know you're going to succeed, and that's a wonderful feeling.

There is just no substitute for hard work. If there's a secret to the most successful people, this is probably it. The person who works the longest and the hardest and with the most intensity is the person who is going to be farthest ahead.

Sacrifice is a part of paying the price. If you're going to make your dreams come true, you are going to have to make sacrifices. If you are going to win, sacrifice can't be just a "sometimes" thing. When things are good, you don't stop paying the price. You don't let up and take time off as soon as you have achieved a little bit of success.

One of the special benefits of paying the price is the satisfaction you feel when you work hard and succeed. You start to feel self-control; you start to create for yourself. You feel good about yourself and it makes you want to even work harder. This extra effort and hard work is all a part of paying the price for success. It's also one of the keys between you being *good* at what you do and being *great* at what you do.

LIFE LESSON 10
MENTORSHIP

This is one of the most important things you can do: find someone who is where you want to be. You might have to pay for his or her time, but it's worth it. Once you have the knowledge, you'll begin saving money and shortening your journey toward success. Don't ever look at the price you have to pay; just look at it as an investment in your life and business.

After you select a mentor, make sure you build a one-on-one relationship. Get his or her phone number, and make sure you do more listening than asking questions.

If there's anything that you want to improve in your life, I suggest you pick a coach to help you along in your journey. Please don't be like me and wait eight years to get a mentor,
because I could have been where I want to be in a shorter time in my life.

ABOUT THE AUTHOR

If pain doesn't lead to humility, you have wasted your suffering.
—Katerina Stoykova Klemer

During my life's tenure, I have grown tremendously. Growing up in rural Arkansas presented many obstacles that I was determined to overcome. I was a premature child weighing one pound; doctors told my mom that I would probably not live to three years of age. From being verbally and physically abused as a child to struggling to develop and maintain a successful business, I know the feeling of triumph very well. In addition, I have witnessed others experience jubilation in surviving nearly fatal events.

Who we are in the present includes who we were in the past.
—Fred Rogers

I received a bachelor's degree in business marketing from the University of Arkansas at Pine Bluff in 2007. Upon completion of my degree, I migrated to Dallas, Texas, where I began my networking endeavors.

The training and experience I received over the last eight years of my life have contributed to my personal and professional growth as a leader and a mentor. My past experiences have imparted knowledge that fuels my passion to help others. As a novice entrepreneur at the age of twenty-two, I was not aware of the mountains I would have to climb.

Renowned speakers and trainers such as Johnny Wimbrey, Les Brown, and Willie Jolley have been major influences in my life.

Therefore I understand the significance of motivating others and serving as a framework for people striving to overcome tasks despite the degree of extremity.

Know who you are, and be it. Know what you want, and go out and get it!
—Carroll Bryant

My ultimate goal, through motivation, is to help as many people as possible, guiding them in realizing the conception of defeat despite their past.

Your mess can become your message!
—Johnny Wimbey

To request Lucas Armstrong to speak at your next event and to learn about other products and services, please visit www.LucasArmstrong.net.